Money Matters

Spending and Saving

By Mary Hill

Children's Press®
A Division of Scholastic Inc.
New York / Toronto / London / Auckland / Sydney
Mexico City / New Delhi / Hong Kong
Danbury, Connecticut

3 1257 01629 7839

Photo Credits: Cover © Photodisc/Getty Images; pp. 5, 21 (top left) © Paul Barton/Corbis; p. 7 © ROB & SAS/Corbis; pp. 9, 21 (top right) © Tom Bean/Corbis; p. 11 © Chip Henderson/Index Stock Imagery, Inc.; pp. 13, 21 (bottom left) © Roy Morsch/Corbis; p. 15 © Paul Barton/Corbis; pp. 17, 21 (bottom right) © Chuck Savage/Corbis; p. 19 © SuperStock
Contributing Editor: Shira Laskin
Book Design: Mindy Liu

Library of Congress Cataloging-in-Publication Data

Hill, Mary, 1977–
        Spending and saving / by Mary Hill.
        p. cm. — (Money matters)
        Includes index.
        ISBN 0-516-25059-0 (lib. bdg.) — ISBN 0-516-25174-0 (pbk.)
        1. Children—Finance, Personal—Juvenile literature. 2. Saving and investment—Juvenile literature. I. Title.

HG179.H473 2005
332—dc22

                                                    2004015805

Contents

There are many kinds of jobs.

Some people work in stores.

Some people work outside.

People can **save** the money they **earn**.

They can save money in a **bank**.

People can save their money in **piggy banks** too.

People can also **spend** their money.

They can spend money on a house.

People also spend money on food.

Sometimes people spend money on **supplies** for school.

19

It is fun to learn about spending and saving money.

21

New Words

bank (**bangk**) a place where people save
their money

earn (**uhrn**) to get money for working at a job or for
working in some other way

piggy banks (**pig**-ee **bangks**) toy banks in the shape
of a pig in which people save coins

save (**sayv**) to keep something because you want to
have it or do something with it later

spend (**spend**) to use

supplies (suh-**plyze**) things needed to do something

To Find Out More

Books
All about Money
by Natalie M. Rosinsky
Compass Point Books

Earning Money
by Tanya Thayer
Lerner Publishing Group

Web Site
Savings Bonds for Kids
http://www.publicdebt.treas.gov/sav/savkids.htm
Learn about saving money and play games on this Web site.

Index

About the Author

Mary Hill is a children's book author. She has written books about many different subjects.

Reading Consultants

Kris Flynn, Coordinator, Small School District Literacy, The San Diego County Office of Education

Shelly Forys, Certified Reading Recovery Specialist, W.J. Zahnow Elementary School, Waterloo, IL

Paulette Mansell, Certified Reading Recovery Specialist, and Early Literacy Consultant, TX